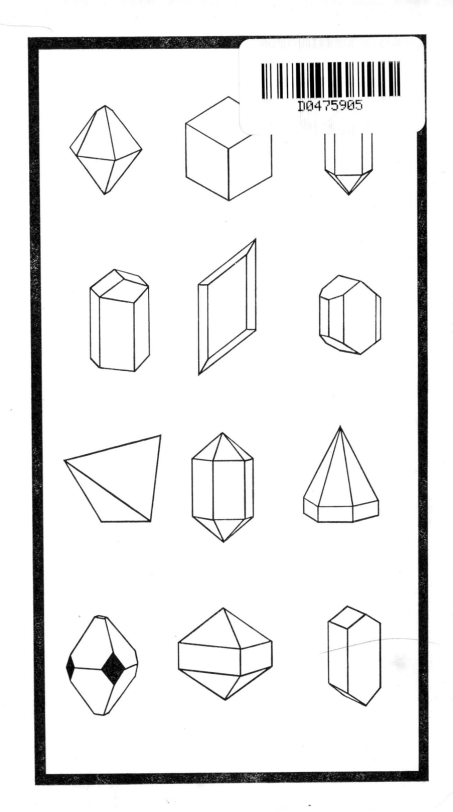

MACDONALD JUNIOR REFERENCE LIBRARY

ROCKS AND
MINERALS

JRL 25

© B.P.C. Publishing Limited 1969
SBN 356 02723 6 (non-net)
SBN 356 02724 4 (net)

MACDONALD JUNIOR REFERENCE LIBRARY

ROCKS
and
MINERALS

MACDONALD EDUCATIONAL
49–50 POLAND STREET, LONDON W.1.

Editor's Note

This book gives a brief account of some of the common rocks and minerals. It tells how they were formed, where they are likely to be found and how man has put them to use over the ages.

Metric Equivalents

1 inch	.	.	.	.	2·54 centimetres
1 foot	.	.	.	.	0·3048 metre
1 yard	.	.	.	.	0·9144 metre

Acknowledgement

The photograph on page 25 of this book is a Crown Copyright Geological survey photograph. Reproduced by permission of the Controller, H.M. Stationery Office.

Contents

The World of Rocks and Minerals ●

Thousands of millions of years ago, the Earth was a mass of boiling, bubbling rock. Solid rocks formed as it cooled down. Then the weather gradually broke down the rocks into pieces, which in time were changed into other types of rock.

Movements inside the Earth twisted and pushed the rocks. They buried some and raised others. In many parts of the world you can see great folds in the rock layers which show you how the Earth's surface was twisted long ago.

As the rocks cooled, the substances inside them became the different forms we call *minerals*. When they cooled slowly, the minerals had time to grow into large and beautiful crystals.

We use rocks and minerals in every branch of our everyday life. For example, we build with limestone and granite rocks, and use slate for the roof and marble for decoration. We make cement out of chalk and bricks out of clay. We wear beautiful mineral crystals as jewels. One mineral, salt, we actually eat. Other minerals we change into the metals which are so important to us for all our equipment and machinery.

This book describes the various kinds of rock and the way in which they were formed. It also describes the most common and the most interesting of the minerals they contain.

Igneous rocks formed when the Earth cooled down. Great heat and pressure changed some of these to metamorphic rock. Fragments from both kinds were carried away and deposited to form sedimentary rock.

Metamorphic rock

Sedimentary rock

● Looking for Rocks and Minerals

The best way of learning about rocks and minerals is to go out into the country or into the mountains and see them for yourself. All you really need is a keen eye. You can see the massive chalk cliffs and the way in which they are made up of layers. You can observe how the rivers have eaten their way through solid rocks, and how the sea has pounded and broken the shore rocks into pebbles and sand.

Almost every rock or stone has an interesting feature, and you will soon learn to recognize interesting specimens. You may even be lucky enough to come across the *fossils*, or remains, of ancient creatures.

A lot can be done, therefore, without any equipment whatsoever, but a little equipment can be very helpful. Probably the most important item is a *geologist's hammer*. This is a little different from a normal hammer. The head is square at one end and pointed at the other. You use this hammer for splitting rocks and for removing crystals from them.

If you wish to collect specimens, you will need a strong rucksack to carry them in. You will also find that a magnifying glass will help to show the beauty and make-up of the rocks to the best advantage.

The geologist at work. He has his hammer and rucksack for collecting rock samples. He marks all the geological features he sees, and the places where the samples are found, on a map.

Recognizing Mineral Specimens ●

After you have collected your specimens of minerals, you must try to decide what they are. It is not always easy to recognize a mineral instantly. First you must do some detective work and look for clues to identify it.

The first clue is *colour*, but this is not very reliable. The mineral fluor-spar, for example, can be found in almost any colour. The *weight*, too, is not always very helpful. A more reliable clue is the *lustre* of the mineral – the way in which it reflects light. Some minerals look almost metal-like, some look glassy, and others look dull.

The shape of the mineral's crystals and the way they break, or *cleave*, will also help to narrow down your search.

Now try some tests on the mineral. If you rub it on a white tile, you find that it leaves a coloured *streak*. The colour of the streak gives another valuable clue to the mineral's identity.

Finding the *hardness* of the mineral helps a lot. You do this by trying to scratch it with several objects whose hardness you know. You can use a fingernail, a coin, a knife-blade, and a piece of glass for testing the hardness. (See page 57.)

After these tests, you should be fairly certain of what the mineral is.

Here are two tests to make on your mineral specimens.

Transparent

Translucent

Opaque

You can arrange your specimens in order of hardness by seeing which scratches others. Galena is softer than calcite so it will be scratched by it; but it is harder than gypsum which it will scratch.

Place each specimen over a mark on a sheet of paper. Those you can see through clearly are transparent. Those you can almost see through are translucent. Those that do not let any light through are opaque.

Calcite scratches galena

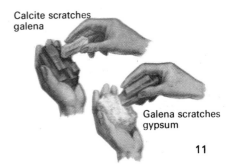

Galena scratches gypsum

11

Rocks and Minerals A to Z

Firefighter in asbestos suit

Weaver at loom

Fireproof material is woven from fibres of rock.

Chrysotile fibres

ASBESTOS If you have seen pictures or a film of firemen fighting a very fierce fire, you may have noticed that some of them were wearing special white suits which did not catch fire. They did not burn because they were made of rock!

Some minerals are found naturally in the form of tiny threads, or fibres. They are all given the name *asbestos.* Most asbestos fibres, like those of cotton and wool, can be spun into yarn and then woven into cloth. This cloth is really made of rock and therefore will not burn.

Asbestos is used for other products which need to withstand heat, such as the linings for the brakes of motor cars and the safety curtains in theatres. It is also used with cement to make roofing materials.

The commonest asbestos mineral is a form of *serpentine* which has grey, silky fibres. The usual form of serpentine is green and mottled like a snake, or serpent.

The magnified photograph shows the fibres in the piece of chrysotile. Crocidolite and amosite are just two of the many other kinds of asbestos mineral.

Chrysotile

Amosite

Crocidolite

BARYTES When you go to the hospital to have your stomach X-rayed, you are given a 'barium meal'. This is a chalky white liquid mixture which makes your insides show up on the X-ray photographs. The liquid is a pure form of the mineral *barytes*. One of the main uses of barytes is in white paints. Barytes may be colourless, white, or tinted yellow or red. It is quite heavy for an earthy mineral. Its name means 'heavy', and it is sometimes called *heavy spar*.

Barytes. This crystal formation is known as a cockscomb spur.

BASALT Several kinds of *igneous rock* are formed when lava cools. (See IGNEOUS ROCK.) *Basalt* is the most widespread of them all. It is a very uninteresting looking rock which is dark and dull. It contains crystals, but they are too tiny to be seen with the naked eye.

The most interesting feature about basalt is that sometimes, on cooling, it splits into massive, many-sided columns. The most spectacular example of these columns is the *Giant's Causeway* in Northern Ireland. According to legend the columns were once supposed to be remains of a structure built by giants to cross over to Scotland.

Columnar basalt. These many-sided columns are formed from hot lava. The rock splits evenly as it cools down slowly and shrinks.

The Giant's Causeway, a spectacular basalt formation.

BAUXITE is the only profitable ore of aluminium, one of the lightest and most important of our metals. Common clay also contains aluminium, but it cannot be extracted easily. Bauxite should really be considered a rock rather than a mineral because it is a mixture of minerals. The important one is *alumina,* an oxide of aluminium. Some bauxite is used in mineral form to make cement, chemicals and *abrasives* – materials used for grinding and polishing. (See CRYOLITE, ORE.)

CALCITE The great chalk and limestone cliffs you have seen at the seaside and elsewhere are made up almost entirely of one mineral, *calcite.* The spectacular stalactites and stalagmites in limestone caves are formed from calcite.

All these forms of calcite are slightly impure. Chalk, the whitest, is the purest form, but limestones may be stained yellow, brown, and even red by impurities. The purest forms of calcite are clear crystals. If you look hard, you can find calcite crystals in many chalk and limestone rocks. They appear in many shapes and sizes; some are squat, others look like sharpened pencils. Some have attractive coloured tints.

The purest form of calcite is called *Iceland Spar.* This crystal literally makes you 'see double'. Place a piece of Iceland Spar over a line of type in a book. You will see two lines when you look through the crystal. This effect is due to an optical property called *polarization.*

Calcite is one of the commonest minerals. It is a carbonate and therefore fizzes when acid is poured onto it. This is a good test for carbonates. (See MINERALS.)

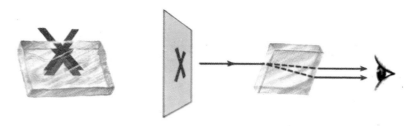

Mark a cross on a sheet of paper. Then place a calcite crystal over it. You will see two crosses because of polarization, or double refraction. The calcite has bent some of the light less than the rest so that you see two images of the cross.

Dredging for cassiterite in Malaya, where most of the world's tin is found.
A dredger is a machine with a moving chain of buckets. It scoops up sand, clay and gravel from the bed of the river or lake. Sometimes they are used to clear a deep channel for shipping. Or, like this one, they bring up valuable placer deposits.

CASSITERITE Practically all the tin we use comes from the ore *cassiterite*, also called *tinstone*. The word 'cassiterite' comes from the name ancient traders gave to the British Isles. They were called the Cassiterides – the 'Tin Islands' – because of the valuable tin mines there.

Cassiterite is usually dark brown or black in colour and is hard and very heavy, almost as heavy as lead in fact. Most cassiterite is found in deposits in gravel and stream beds, called *placers*. (See PLACERS.) It is usually mined by dredging.

CHALK is a pure kind of limestone which is dazzlingly white when freshly cut. (See LIMESTONE.) It is very soft and is not a suitable building stone. Most chalk deposits contain round lumps of a much harder material called *flint*. (See FLINT.) The 'chalk' used for writing on blackboards is not really chalk at all, but a form of another mineral, gypsum.

Chalk cliffs at Beachy Head, Sussex. Chalk is a soft rock and the sea wears away the base of the cliff. Then the unsupported rock higher up collapses. The sea dissolves the chalk, leaving pieces of flint and hard rock on the beach.

CLAY The geologist classes *clay* as a rock because it forms a large part of the Earth's crust, but it is not hard and strong like granite. It is soft and weak and consists of very fine grains loosely packed together.

The nearest clay comes to being 'hard as a rock' is when it is baked. Baking, or 'firing', turns clay into bricks, our most common building material. The firing is usually done in a huge oven called a *kiln*. In some countries where there is very little rain houses are built with sun-dried bricks containing straw. In Egypt, for example, this method has been used for thousands of years.

Most clays are grey, brown, or red, but the purest clay is white. It is called *china-clay*, or *kaolin*. This is the clay used in making all our fine pottery. It is also used in paper-making to produce smooth paper and in the manufacture of paints, soaps, powders, and medical poultices.

Most clays are formed when certain kinds of rock crumble away under the action of the weather, for example. China-clay is formed when hot gases from inside the Earth react chemically with granite and decompose it, or break it down.

A china-clay pit in Cornwall. The white, cone-shaped hills are distinctive landmarks. They are 'tips' or heaps of unwanted material, such as rocks and impurities. It is all dug out of the pit and then separated from the pure clay. You can also tell when you are near a clay pit because everything is covered with fine white dust. Contrast this with a coal-mining area where there are black slag heaps and a film of coal dust everywhere.

The gigantic trees that have become our coal grew in swamps that might have looked like this.

COAL The hard, black *coal* we burn in our grates is a special kind of rock. Most rocks are formed from matter which came from within the Earth, or *inorganic* matter. But coal is a rock which is made up of decayed plants, or *organic* matter. It is found in layers, or *seams*, in some sedimentary rocks and is generally regarded as a sedimentary rock itself. It is also often called a mineral.

Coal is very important to our way of life. We burn it on the fire to give us heat. Power stations burn it to produce electricity. Gasworks burn it to make *gas* and *coke*. Manufacturers produce a wide range of chemicals from coal, including aspirins, plastics, and dyes, and there are hundreds of other uses.

Two hundred and fifty million years ago, parts of the Earth were covered with swamps and giganitic plants. Ferns grew as high as trees do today. When the plants died, they fell to the bottom of the swamps and decayed. Deposits of mud formed over them. More plants grew and decayed and were buried under mud. Over the years, the mud became rock and the layers of decayed plants became coal seams.

If you look closely at a piece of coal, you can often see the *fossils*, or remains, of the leaves of the giant ferns.

Seams of coal are found in layers sandwiched between other kinds of rock.

COAL
GANNISTER
SANDSTONE
SHALE
COAL
GANNISTER

Another coal seam formed
The land rose and more swamps grew up
The water deposited sand over the mud
Mud buried them
The trees and plants died and decayed
Grit was deposited at the bottom of swamps

COAL-MINING – digging coal from the ground – is a very big industry. Some coal is mined on the surface, but most of it is mined underground. The main kinds of coal are brown coal, or lignite, bituminous coal, and anthracite. Lignite is soft and dull. Bituminous coal is partly shiny but dull in patches. Anthracite is quite hard and shiny.

This diagram of a coal mine shows some of the machinery and the way it is used to bring us coal from the depths of the earth.

KEY

1 Pit head of shaft
2 Winding ropes
3 Cage going down
4 Guide rails
5 Main roads
6 Coal tubs going to cage
7 Air pressure machinery room
8 Locomotive pulling tubs
9 Underground manager's office
10 Conveyor belt loading
11 Drilling for explosives
12 Mechanical cutter
13 Men at work with picks
14 Conveyor filling tubs

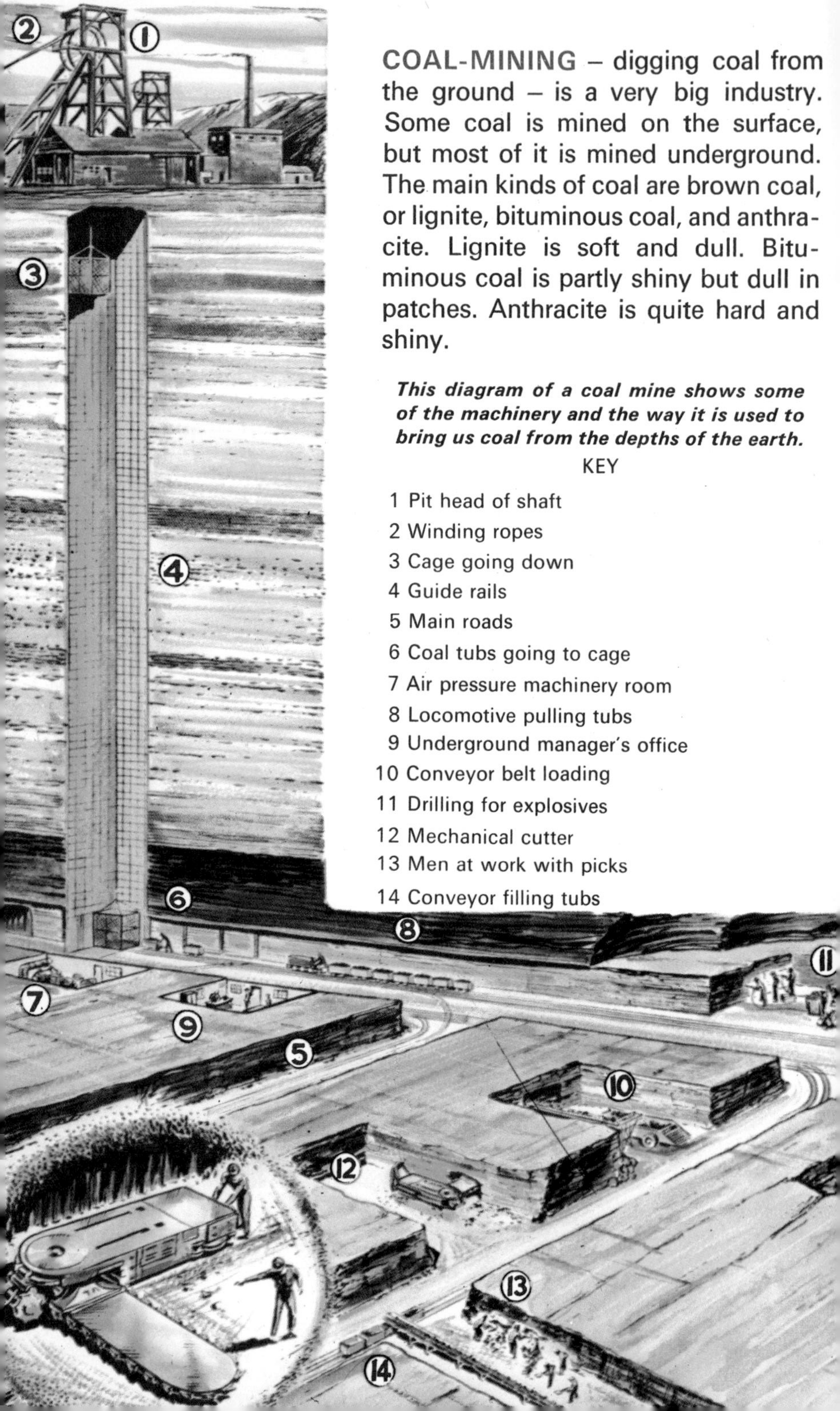

CONGLOMERATE is one of the easiest rocks to recognize. It is often called *puddingstone* because it looks very much like a rock 'pudding'. It consists of gravel, pebbles, and even large boulders, which are cemented, or bound, together with hard sand or clay. *Breccia* is a similar rock but contains sharp pieces of rock instead of pebbles. Both conglomerate and breccia are sedimentary rocks.

Conglomerate is sometimes called 'puddingstone' because the smooth pieces of rock in it look like currants in a pudding. The pieces may be any size, from fine gravel to huge round boulders, but they have all been ground smooth in water.

Breccia contains sharp pieces of broken rock cemented together like the pebbles in conglomerate. The name breccia comes from an Italian word meaning fragments of masonry, or building stone.

COPPER ORES Copper is one of the few metals which can be found *native* in the ground. (See METALS.) The most important sources of this metal are its compounds. Copper forms a larger group of minerals than any other metal. Several hundreds have been found and many of them are useful ores. (See ORE.)

Copper is a very useful metal. It is used by itself, and also when it has been combined with other metals in *alloys*, such as bronze and brass. For instance, it is made into copper wire, copper pipes, bronze coins and brass ornaments.

There are copper mines in many parts of the world. One of the most important producers is the Copper Belt in Africa. There are also huge mines in Canada and the United States.

Tetrahedrite

Malachite

Chalcopyrite

These are three of the minerals which contain copper; chalcopyrite, tetrahedrite, malachite. Chalcopyrite is the most common ore mineral of copper. It is sometimes called copper pyrites.

The most common ore mineral is *chalcopyrite*, or *copper pyrites*, which contains both iron and copper sulphides. It has a beautiful deep yellow colour, which may flash all colours of the rainbow like a peacock's feathers. For this reason, chalcopyrite is sometimes called 'peacock ore'. It is sometimes confused with iron pyrites, which looks very similar. Both minerals have often been mistaken for gold and have earned the name *fool's gold*.

Chalcocite is also a sulphide ore but it is black. *Cuprite* is a reddish-brown oxide ore, which is sometimes called 'ruby copper' because of its appearance.

The two most colourful copper ores are *azurite* and *malachite*, both carbonates. Azurite is a deep, rich, blue colour. Malachite is a deep green. The green deposit, or *patina*, which you often see on copper and bronze statues and ornaments is a thin coating of malachite.

Ruby

Sapphire

CORUNDUM You would hardly think that a fiery red ruby, a brilliant blue sapphire, and a grinding wheel have much in common, but they have. They are all different forms of the very hard mineral *corundum*, which is second only to diamond in hardness.

Ruby and *sapphire* are rare and valuable crystal forms of corundum. (See GEMS.) The grinding wheel is made of the common dull-grey form of the mineral.

Corundum makes an excellent *abrasive*, or grinding material, because it is so hard. Sometimes it is found mixed with the mineral magnetite, and the mixture is called *emery*. Powdered emery is glued onto paper and cloth to make the familiar *emery paper* or *emery cloth* we use to smooth down metal surfaces.

This dull-grey grinding wheel is also made of corundum although it does not look at all like ruby or sapphire.

CRYOLITE is a fascinating mineral. Its name means 'frost stone'. If you drop a piece of it into a glass of water, it practically disappears! It does this because it refracts, or bends, light rays in almost exactly the same way as water. This means that, as far as your eye is concerned, there appears to be nothing but water in the glass. Another interesting feature about cryolite is that it melts easily, even in a match flame.

The main use of cryolite is in making aluminium. It is used to dissolve the aluminium ore before smelting. Cryolite itself is a compound of aluminium. Greenland is the only place where it is found in large quantities.

CRYSTALS If you look closely at some common table salt, you will notice that it is made up of a very large number of tiny, sparkling cubes, or *crystals*. Salt is one of the many common minerals which *crystallize*, or form crystals. (For some of the crystal shapes see Endpapers.)

Each mineral forms a different kind of crystal. Some form cubic crystals, like salt, some form 'dog-tooth'

Rock salt (halite)

The crystals of rock salt are perfect cubes. We eat this mineral as table salt.

Some minerals grow in these crystal shapes.

Fluorite

Apatite

Realgar

Gold

Mispickel

Prism-shaped crystals of mispickel, which is an ore containing iron and arsenic.

Aragonite

The sharp-pointed crystals of aragonite often form pairs, called twins. Sometimes they grow in groups so that they seem to be hexagonal or six-sided. Crystal shapes are often misleading and have to be examined very carefully, with a microscope, before you can be certain how they were built.

crystals, like calcite; and others form flat, flaky crystals, like mica. The crystals may be colourless or any colour of the rainbow. Some minerals always have crystals of the same colour, but others have crystals of many colours. For example, one of the commonest minerals, quartz, forms pink, 'smoky' yellow and brown, golden, violet and clear crystals. Crystals have been well named 'the flowers of the mineral kingdom'.

The most spectacular examples of mineral crystals are the precious stones, or *gems*, such as diamonds and rubies. Semi-precious gems, such as the coloured quartz crystals, are also valued for their beauty. (See GEMS.)

Wulfenite

Wulfenite often has tabular crystals; that is flat, like a tablet or tabletop.

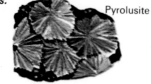

Strontianite

Strontianite has six-sided, pencil-shaped crystals. Quartz crystals also grow in this shape.

Pyrolusite is a mineral containing manganese. These star-shaped clusters are made up of needle-like crystals.

Pyrolusite

DIAMOND is the hardest of all the minerals and the most valued of all the precious stones, or *gems*, used in jewellery. When cut and polished, diamond is the most brilliant of them all. (See GEMS.)

Some of the most famous diamonds in the world form part of the British Crown Jewels. They include the *Koh-i-noor* ('mountain of light') ; the *First Star of Africa*, which is set in the Sceptre with the Cross; and the *Second Star of Africa*, which is set in the Imperial State Crown. The Stars of Africa came from the world's biggest diamond, the *Cullinan*, which weighed nearly one and a half pounds.

In its natural state, diamond is sometimes covered in a dull grey film. In this form it is called a *rough diamond*. The rough diamond is cut with a great many flat sides, or *facets*, to produce the greatest possible brilliance. The cut diamond sparkles all colours of the rainbow. The 'cutting' and polishing of the facets is done by grinding, with discs coated with diamond dust. Diamond is so hard that the only material which will cut it is itself !

Not all rough diamonds, however, are suitable for cutting and polishing into fine gems. They are used in industry as *abrasives* (grinding materials) and for the *bits* (tips) of rock drills. They are called *industrial diamonds*.

Diamond is a pure crystal form of carbon. Graphite is the other natural form of pure carbon. It is almost unbelievable that diamond and graphite are really the same substance. Diamond is the hardest and most brilliant mineral, but graphite is one of the softest and dullest. (See GRAPHITE.)

Uncut diamonds. When they have been cut and polished, these precious gems will shine and sparkle even more. The most perfect stones may be set in beautiful jewellery with other gems. Others may be used as industrial diamonds in drilling or grinding tools.

FELDSPAR is the most common and widespread of all minerals. Several kinds of feldspar are found in the form of crystals in granite and other igneous rocks. The crystals may be white, pink, green or blue. Large amounts of feldspar are used for making pottery and glass. The feldspar is mined from deposits of pegamatite, which is a form of granite containing large crystals.

Feldspars are the commonest of the silicate minerals. (See SILICA AND SILICATES.) They break down under the action of the weather to form a variety of clays, including the very useful china-clay.

Feldspar minerals are very common in igneous rocks. There are many kinds of different colours. This green variety is sometimes called Amazonstone.

Flint breaks in smooth curves with sharp edges. This made it useful to prehistoric man, who used it as tools and weapons.

Flint scraper

FLINT can be found in the form of rounded lumps in most deposits of chalk, but it is totally different from chalk both in appearance and in make-up. Flint is black or grey, and is a form of the common mineral silica. Like chalk, flint comes from the remains of tiny sea creatures.

Flint is very hard indeed. It does not split when struck, but chips in smooth curves. Prehistoric man used it for thousands of years to make both weapons and tools. You can see fine examples of them in most museums. Today, flint is used mainly for road-making and building.

FLUORESCENT MINERALS Some minerals glow in the dark when certain kinds of invisible light are shone on them. They are called *fluorescent* minerals, after fluor-spar, which shows this

Cubic crystals of fluor-spar in ordinary light.

The same crystals fluorescing when ultra-violet light is shone on them.

property. Ultra-violet light is the invisible light normally used. This is the light in sunshine which gives you your tan.

Some minerals, called *phosphorescent* minerals, continue to glow after the light is removed. They are named after a chemical element called phosphorus, which glows in the dark.

Besides fluor-spar, two of the best known fluorescent minerals are *scheelite*, a tungsten ore, and *willemite*, a zinc ore. Some specimens of diamond, calcite and opal also fluoresce. Some willemite is also phosphorescent.

FLUOR-SPAR (also called FLUOR-ITE) is a beautiful and interesting mineral that can be made to glow in the dark. Some specimens of fluor-spar glow with a blue light when invisible light such as ultra-violet light is shone on them. Fluor-spar lends its name to this effect, called *fluorescence*. (See FLUORESCENT MINERALS.) When fluor-spar is gently heated, it gives off a pale greenish glow.

Fluor-spar crystallizes in perfect cubes, which may be colourless, yellow, brown, green, purple, and blue. A banded blue variety is called *Blue John*. It was once used for carving ornaments.

Blue John vase carved from fluor-spar.

Today, most fluor-spar is used in steel-making furnaces to make the materials melt more easily. Some is used to provide the 'fluoride' for some kinds of toothpaste and drinking water.

Fossil of a trilobite. These creatures used to live in the seas millions of years ago, but they have long been extinct.

Fossil of a piece of the giant horsetail plant. It is found in coal seams because these plants grew in the swamps millions of years ago.

FOSSILS Most of our knowledge about life in past ages has been obtained by studying plant and animal remains preserved in rocks. These remains are called *fossils*.

Some fossils are the actual bones of creatures such as the dinosaurs – the 'terrible lizards'. Some are merely moulds which formed around the dead creature before it decayed. Others are *petrified* fossils – fossils which have literally changed into stone over the years. Petrified forests are fossils of this kind. (See PETRIFIED WOOD.)

Almost all fossils come from sedimentary rocks. Any remains in the other kinds of rock would have been

Ammonite fossils can be any size, from several feet across down to a fraction of an inch.

Graptolite fossils. They are probably moulds of the skeletons of tiny creatures.

A polished slab of fossilized limestone from Derbyshire. The rock is actually made of the shells and bodies of millions of sea-creatures. As they died and fell to the sea bed their remains were buried and cemented into solid rock.

destroyed by heat when the rocks were formed. Some of the best fossils are to be found in limestones. Some limestones, such as coral, are themselves made up of the bodies of ancient sea creatures. (See LIMESTONE.) Some of the commonest fossils in limestones are brachiopods. They can be seen clearly in many limestone beds.

Coal is a special kind of sedimentary rock in which you can often see the impression of the leaves of plants which lived millions of years ago.

GALENA is by far the richest source of lead. It often contains valuable traces of silver as an 'impurity'. Galena is very soft and very heavy. It can easily be broken into tiny cubes. It is almost the same colour as lead itself. Like many other metal ores, galena is a sulphide. (See ORE.)

This mass of galena crystals has been drawn enlarged to show their cubic structure, or shape.

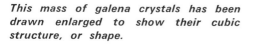

GEMS Occasionally, Nature produces minerals of such exceptional beauty that we use them as jewellery. We call these minerals *gems*, or *precious stones*. The finest gems, *diamond*, *ruby*, *emerald*, and *sapphire*, are very rare and therefore very valuable. The greatest jewellery in the world sparkles with the brilliance of diamonds, the fiery red of rubies, and the purest greens and blues of emeralds and sapphires.

The value of a gem depends not only on its beauty and rarity but also on its hardness. There is no point in using a beautiful stone in a ring if the stone can be scratched easily. It would soon lose its beauty. The four main gems are so valuable because they combine great beauty and rarity with great hardness. Diamond is the hardest of them all.

Not all gems, however, are stones. Beautiful, milky white *pearls*, for rings and necklaces, are made within the bodies of shellfish called *pearl oysters*. *Amber* is a yellowish-brown gem which is formed from the hardened sap of ancient pine trees. It is called a *fossil resin*.

Other gems are attractive, but less hard and more common than the true gems. Therefore they are not as valuable. They are usually called *semi-precious* gems or stones. Among them are certain varieties of *quartz* and the *garnets* found in the rock gneiss. (See GNEISS, QUARTZ.)

The beauty and brilliance of a gem can be increased by carefully *cutting* and *polishing* the natural crystals. Any flaws in the surface can be removed at the same time. Cutting and polishing is a highly skilled art. For each gem, there are particular cuts which bring out the beauty to the greatest extent. The gems may be cut with many flat sides, or *facets*, or with a smooth, rounded face. The *brilliant* cut of a diamond has 58 facets.

Emerald in quartz

Cut emerald

Cut diamonds

Diamond is a rare crystal form of the chemical element *carbon*. (See DIAMOND.) Ruby and sapphire are different coloured crystal forms of the mineral *corundum*. (See CORUNDUM.) Emerald is the rarest and most valued crystal form of the mineral *beryl*. Another crystal form of beryl is the gem *aquamarine*, which is bluish-green. *Topaz* is another valuable gem which may be colourless, yellow, blue or pink.

All these gems are different kinds of crystals. Several gems are *opaque*, they do not let light through. The most outstanding one is *opal*. It does not really have any colour of its own, except as a background. But it shimmers and gleams with changing patterns of every colour. *Turquoise* is another opaque gem. It is bluish-green with a beautiful spider's-web pattern on it.

Gems have always been regarded as lucky charms because of their beauty and rarity. For each month of the year there is a gem called a *birthstone*. Wearing the stone of your birth month is supposed to bring you good luck. For a list of the birthstones, see page 58.

Gems: some of the world's most precious minerals. As they look when they are found, and after they have been cut and polished for use as ornaments and jewellery.

Rough opal

Polished opal

Ruby crystal

Cut ruby

Topaz

Uncut diamond

Jade

Carved and polished jade ornament

GEOLOGY is the science which deals with changes in the Earth's crust. *Geologists* are the people who study geology. They study the way in which the Earth developed; how the land masses and the seas were formed; and how the mountain ranges and valleys appeared. They observe how the weather breaks some rocks down and how other rocks form from the fragments.

Geologists also study the nature and make-up of the rocks and minerals which form the Earth's crust. The study of rocks is called *petrology*, and the study of minerals is called *mineralogy*. This book deals mainly with these two branches of geology.

Mica schist is a meta-morphic rock contain-ing glittering flakes of mica.

Close-up showing 'plates' of mica in mica schist

GNEISS (pronounced *nice*) is a rock in which the minerals are arranged in quite thick, light-and-dark bands. The main minerals in gneiss are quartz, feldspar, and mica, the same minerals as those found in granite. Some gneiss is indeed formed from granite. Great heat and pressure within the Earth squeeze and stretch the minerals in granite into layers. Gneiss, then, is a metamorphic rock.

When the layers of minerals are thin the rock is called a *schist.* The minerals are present as flaky layers, which can easily be separated. *Mica schist* is a schist which contains a large amount of thin, glistening sheets of mica. Many specimens of schist and gneiss are studded with tiny, dark red crystals of *garnet.* Garnets are semi-precious stones, or *gems*. (See GEMS.)

GRANITE is one of our best-known rocks. It is an attractive rock, especially when polished. For this reason, it is widely used for building monuments and for 'facing' buildings. In appearance, granite is fairly light with coloured speckles. If you look closely, you can see that the speckles are actually masses of tiny crystals.

The main crystals in granite are feldspar, which may be white, grey, or pink, and transparent quartz. Tiny black specks of mica scattered among the other crystals give granite a 'sparkle'.

Red granite

Pegmatite

Granite is an igneous rock. It is one of the most widespread of the Earth's rocks. Most of it lies deep beneath the surface where it was formed when molten rock cooled. (See IGNEOUS ROCK.)

Pegmatite is a rock that contains the same kinds of crystal as granite but they are very much larger.

Gabbro is an igneous rock which is much darker and heavier than granite because it often contains dark green minerals. It also contains feldspar.

GRAPHITE The black 'lead' of the pencils you write with is not made from lead at all, but from *graphite*, mixed with clay. Graphite is one of the softest of minerals and feels 'greasy' to the touch. Some machinery is in fact 'greased' with it.

Although they do not look alike, graphite is chemically the same as diamond, which is the hardest substance known. Graphite and diamond are both forms of pure carbon. The difference between them arises from a difference in the structure of their crystals. Diamond forms strong transparent crystals, while graphite crystallizes in thin black flakes.

Graphite is found mainly in metamorphic rocks such as gneiss and schist. It probably came originally from vegetable matter which was trapped in the rock layers and changed by great heat and pressure. This process is called *metamorphosis*.

Graphite, which is sometimes called black-lead. It is a good conductor of heat. It feels cold if you touch it because it quickly takes the heat away from your finger. It also feels slippery and greasy because its flat, scaly crystals slide over each other easily. This property makes it ideal for lubricating, or 'greasing' machinery so that moving parts can slip over each other more easily.

GYPSUM You have probably handled a piece of *gypsum* quite often, because blackboard 'chalk' is made of gypsum. Like chalk, gypsum is white and quite soft. If you have broken an arm or a leg, you will also have met gypsum in another form – *plaster of Paris*. This is used for making plaster casts of all kinds. Gypsum is also used by builders to make many kinds of plasters and wall coverings.

Plaster of Paris is made by heating gypsum. When water is added to it, it can be moulded into any shape, but it soon dries and hardens.

Gypsum is found in sedimentary beds, formed when sea water dried up. Sometimes it is found as large clear crystals. It is also found in a hard form we call *alabaster*. This can be carved into attractive statues and ornaments.

These needle-like crystals are one of the less common forms of gypsum. You may find it as satin spar, which has long, silky fibres. Gypsum is one of the minerals in which the crystals sometimes grow in pairs, or twins.

IGNEOUS ROCK Molten rock called *magma* lies deep within the Earth. It cools when it comes near or to the surface to form a class of rock called *igneous rock*. *Igneous* means 'made by fire'. Igneous rocks were the first ones formed when the Earth cooled from a molten mass.

The igneous rocks formed from magma reaching the surface are different from those formed below ground. Magma forces its way out of the ground from volcanoes, and is then known as *lava.* (See LAVA.)

Lava which cools very quickly forms a kind of natural glass called *obsidian,* or a greyish rock with air bubbles in it called *pumice.* (See OBSIDIAN, PUMICE.) If the lava cools a little more slowly, the rock formed contains fine crystals of minerals. *Basalt* is a rock of this kind. (See BASALT.)

Magma which stays beneath the ground forces its way into other rocks before it cools down. Igneous rocks formed in this way cool very slowly. The minerals they contain have time to grow into quite large crystals before the rock hardens. You

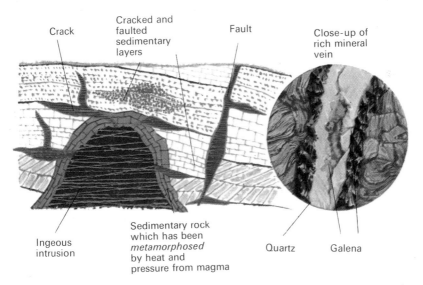

Crack

Cracked and faulted sedimentary layers

Fault

Close-up of rich mineral vein

Ingeous intrusion

Sedimentary rock which has been *metamorphosed* by heat and pressure from magma

Quartz

Galena

Molten rock, called magma, cools when it comes from the depths and forces its way up to, and out of the surface of the earth. The magma cools to become igneous rock. The rock body is called an igneous intrusion.

Liquid from the magma flows into cracks and faults in the surrounding rocks. It contains solutions of valuable minerals. When it cools, these form rich mineral veins. Right: a crack lined with galena and a vein of quartz. Galena is rich in lead and silver.

can see the crystals clearly with the naked eye. *Granite* is one of the best known igneous rocks of this kind.

Solutions of minerals travel along with the magma beneath the ground. When the magma has cooled and hardened, the solutions penetrate cracks in the surrounding rocks and leave rich mineral *veins*. These veins provide us with many of our most valuable ore deposits, including those of gold, silver, and lead.

Flakes of gold in quartzite.

Quartz veins in gabbro.

33

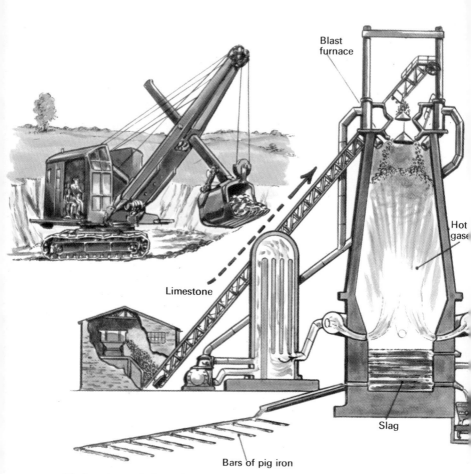

- Blast furnace
- Hot gases
- Limestone
- Slag
- Bars of pig iron

Pig iron is made from iron ore by a process called smelting. The iron ore is mixed with limestone and put in a very hot blast furnace. The materials in the ore that are not wanted mix with the lime and float to the surface as slag. This leaves the pure molten iron which is run off into troughs. It cools to form solid bars of iron, called pigs. Pig iron is refined to make an even more useful metal, steel.

IRON ORES Iron and steel are our most important metals. Millions of tons of *iron ore* are needed every year to supply the giant iron- and steel-making furnaces. Fortunately there are large and widespread deposits of the various iron ores. The main ones are haematite, magnetite, limonite, all forms of iron oxides, and the clay-ironstones, which contain iron carbonate. (See ORE.)

Haematite is usually blood-red in colour. Its name comes from the Greek word for blood. Sometimes it is found in rounded, kidney-shaped lumps and is then called 'kidney ore.' Often it occurs in the form of grey or black, mirror-like crystals.

Magnetite, the richest iron ore, looks black and metallic. It is a powerful natural magnet which can pick up pieces of iron and steel. A piece of magnetite can be used as a compass needle. This property gives the mineral its other name, *lodestone* (guiding stone).

Limonite is yellowish-brown in colour. It is often found in marshes and shallow lakes and is sometimes called *bog iron ore.* The yellowish-brown colour of sand, clay, and many other rocks is caused by 'staining' by limonite.

Clay-ironstones are rock-like masses which contain the carbonate mineral *siderite*. They do not contain nearly as much iron as the other ores, but they are important ores in countries such as Britain which have only a few rich ore deposits.

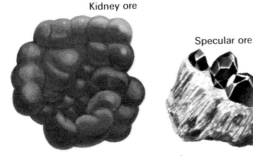

Magnetite is a naturally magnetic iron ore.

Iron pyrites is such a bright shining yellow that it is sometimes called fool's gold.

Kidney ore

Specular ore

Limonite is sometimes called bog iron ore because it is found in swampy ground.

These are two kinds of haematite. Kidney ore is red and rounded; specular ore has shiny black crystals.

35

When a volcano erupts, rivers of molten rock, or lava, flow downhill burning everything in their path. The air is filled with steam, gas and flying pieces of exploding rocks.

The lava cools and forms igneous rock. If it cools quickly, it becomes the glassy rock, obsidian. If it cools slowly, crystals have time to grow and the rock basalt forms.

Lava is full of minerals and these are washed out to make very rich soil. Each time the volcano erupts, the lava forms another layer of rock on the cone of the volcano. It gradually grows higher and higher unless a very violent eruption breaks off large pieces of the mountain.

LAVA is the molten rock which pours out of volcanoes when they erupt. A swift-moving river of red-hot lava is one of the most spectacular sights Nature has to offer. It can also be extremely dangerous. The ancient Roman city of Pompeii was destroyed by streams of lava from Vesuvius.

When lava cools, it forms into a number of kinds of igneous rock. The exact kind formed depends on the rate at which the lava cools. Glass-like *obsidian*, porous *pumice*, and *basalt* are igneous rocks formed from lava. Molten rock which has not reached the surface gives rise to other kinds of igneous rock, including granite. (See IGNEOUS ROCK.)

LIMESTONE is an extremely useful rock. Very large amounts of it are crushed and used to make the cement we need for building. It is also used in the manufacture of iron and steel to take out impurities from the metals. It is most useful as a building stone because it is strong and can be easily cut and carved.

There are several kinds of limestone, varying in colour from pure white to a dirty brown. The purest white form is usually known as *chalk*. All kinds consist almost entirely of one mineral, *calcite*, or a very similar mineral, *dolomite*.

If you visit a limestone region, you will notice that the rock is made up of a number of parallel layers. It is a typical sedimentary rock, formed when layer upon layer of material is deposited and pressed together. These deposits form in two main ways.

Water running over rocks containing calcite will gradually dissolve it and carry it away, say, to a lake. Some creatures in the water may use the dissolved lime to make their hard shells. When the creatures die their shells fall to the lake bottom and build up into a thick deposit.

Sometimes the lake dries up, and the dissolved lime is left as a deposit. It is formed in the same way as the 'fur' in a kettle of water. When you boil the water, the minerals in it are deposited as a fur.

You will not find many surface streams in a limestone region. Instead, there are underground streams, caves and holes, called pot-holes. Water gradually dissolves away the rock, enlarges cracks in them, and disappears underground. In the underground caves there are massive limestone columns

This flat limestone 'plateau' was once the sea-bed. The inland cliff of limestone is called an escarpment.

A close-up picture of oolitic limestone. This kind of rock is called oolite, which means 'egg-stone' because the grains look like fish eggs. Here you can see some of the grains cut in half.
Each grain of sand has been coated with layer upon layer of limestone as it rolled about on the sea bed. This happened in shallow seas where a large amount of the mineral calcium was dissolved in the water.

37

hanging from the roof and rising from the floor. They are called *stalactites* and *stalagmites*. They are formed by the constant dripping of water containing dissolved lime.

MARBLE is one of our most beautiful rocks. The ancient Greeks and Romans carved their statues and built their magnificent temples from fine marble, and it is still a favourite material for the artist and the architect.

Marble is formed when limestone is changed by heat and pressure deep within the Earth. It is therefore a metamorphic rock. The soft, chalky fragments of the mineral calcite in the limestone have been changed into large crystals in the marble. This gives marble its 'sparkle'. The pressure has freed the marble from *faults*, or cracks, and made it hard. For this reason, it can be highly polished.

The best marble is pure white. One of the finest kinds is Carrara marble from Italy. The 'smoky' traces and attractive coloured 'swirls' in most common kinds of marble are caused by impurities which were present in the original limestone.

Some so-called marbles are, in fact, limestones which have been highly polished.

The Taj Mahal, which is in India, is one of the world's most beautiful buildings. It is built of pure, white, Makrana marble.

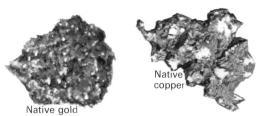

Native copper

Native gold

Some metals which can be found uncombined, or native.

Cinnabar (mercury)

Chromite (chromium)

Wolframite, which is a combination of tungsten, iron and manganese.

METALS Only a few metals are found in their familiar metal form in the Earth's crust. They are called *native* metals. They include gold, silver, copper, and platinum. These metals can be found native because they do not *react*, or combine, with other chemical elements very readily.

Most metals, such as iron and aluminium, react readily with other elements, such as oxygen, to form compounds. So we find them in the ground as compounds. The mineral haematite, for example, is made up of a compound of iron and oxygen. It is called an *ore* of iron because the metal can be extracted from it. (See ORE.) Both the native metals and the ore minerals are known as *metallic minerals*.

Gold, silver, and platinum are known as *precious* metals because they are rare and therefore expensive. They are often used for making jewellery. Gold, for example, can be beaten into very thin 'leaf' for decoration. Much gold and platinum is mined from deposits in stream beds called *placers*. (See PLACERS.)

Most silver is obtained, not as the native metal, but combined with sulphur in the ore argentite. Most copper, too, is obtained from sulphide ores, such as chalcopyrite. Copper is used in coins, cooking vessels, and ornaments, and as wire in electrical equipment.

METAMORPHIC ROCK The rocks which make up the Earth's crust are continually undergoing change. Some rocks are changed by coming into contact with molten rock. Others are changed by the great heat and pressure caused by movements in the crust. Rocks changed in both these ways are called *metamorphic rocks. Metamorphic* means 'changed in form'.

The two other kinds of rock – igneous and sedimentary – may undergo changes and become metamorphic rocks. Then the speckled igneous rock, granite, becomes a banded rock, gneiss, and the dull sedimentary rock, limestone, becomes a shining rock, marble. The changes in appearance are caused by the earrangement and new growth of the mineral crystals in the rocks. Sometimes, entirely new minerals may be formed by metamorphic changes. (See GNEISS, MARBLE, SLATE.)

Few fossils can be found in metamorphic rocks because they are usually destroyed by the great heat and pressure involved.

Slate

Great pressure changes the sedimentary rock shale into the meta-morphic rock slate. Great heat changes limestone into marble.

Marble

A meteorite from outer space.

METEORITE Most rocks were formed deep down within the Earth, but some have come to us from outer space. They are called *meteorites* because they are the remains of *meteors*, or shooting stars. Meteorites are very rare because most meteors are quite small and burn up as they come through the Earth's atmosphere at high speed. There are two main kinds of meteorites. *Stony* meteorites are similar to heavy rocks on Earth. *Iron* meteorites mainly contain a metal mixture, or *alloy*, of iron and nickel.

MICA The sparkling 'frost' on Christmas trees and Christmas cards, and on some fancy wallpapers is a powdered form of the mineral *mica*. Most mica is used in its natural form of transparent, flaky sheets which can easily be separated.

Mica sheet is widely used in electrical equipment as an *insulator*, that is, a substance which does not *conduct* (pass on) electricity. It is by far the best insulator there is.

'Plates' of mica. Mica feels warm when you touch it because it is a good insulator and does not take heat away from your finger.

The thin sheets of mica are very flexible and elastic; they can be bent this way and that and always return to their original position. Thick crystals of mica are made up of many of these sheets and are often referred to as 'books'.

Mica is found widely in the mineral kingdom. It forms the glistening specks in granite and bands in gneiss and mica schist. Most commercial supplies of mica come from bodies of pegmatite, which is a form of granite with huge crystals.

MINERALS The Earth's crust is made up of many different kinds of rocks. The rocks themselves are made up of collections of substances called *minerals*.

Minerals, like everything else on Earth, are composed of certain basic chemical units, or *elements*. The common mineral quartz, for example, is made up of a certain amount of the element silicon and a certain amount of the element oxygen. Quartz will always contain the same relative amounts of these elements.

Some minerals consist of only one element. They are often called *native* elements. They include the metals gold, silver, copper and platinum, and the non-metals graphite and diamond,

Native sulphur. It is a mineral consisting of just the one element, sulphur.

RB–RM–D

Stibnite is a sulphide ore. It contains the metal antimony, combined with sulphur. It is the chief source of this metal.

Chrysotile is a silicate. It contains magnesium combined with silicon and oxygen.

Uraninite, also called pitchblende, is the oxide ore of uranium. It is a very important mineral because it is radioactive.
Radioactive minerals are extremely valuable as a source of atomic power.

This is the carbonate compound of barium.

which are both forms of the element carbon.

Most minerals consist of two or more elements. Often a *metallic* element, such as iron, is combined with a *non-metallic* element, such as oxygen or sulphur. Minerals that are compounds of metal and oxygen are very common. They are called *oxides*. Minerals containing metals combined with sulphur are called *sulphides*. They are also very common. Iron oxides and sulphides, for example, are found throughout the world.

Metallic elements will also combine with groups of other elements to form minerals. The commonest groups are the *silicates* and the *carbonates*. The silicates contain silicon combined with oxygen. Clays are complicated aluminium silicates. The carbonates contain carbon combined with oxygen. Common chalk and limestone are forms of calcium carbonate.

You will notice that the element oxygen appears a lot here. This is not surprising because it is the most common element in the Earth's crust. Silicon is the next most common.

Many of the minerals which contain metallic elements can be treated so that the pure metal can be extracted from them. These minerals are called *ores*. They are very important because we rely so much on metals for making the things we use. (See ORE.)

A great many of the minerals can be found in beautiful crystals of a variety of shapes and sizes. The hardest and rarest of these crystals are used in jewellery. They are known as precious stones, or *gems*. The diamond, the hardest substance on Earth, is the most precious gem. (See CRYSTALS, GEMS.)

The hardness of a mineral and the shape of its crystals often help to identify the mineral. Other aids to recognizing a mineral include its colour, its lustre, or surface appearance, and its weight. (For further details about identifying minerals, see 'Recognizing Mineral Specimens' on page 11.)

MINING AND QUARRYING Vast quantities of minerals and rocks are taken from the ground every year. Taking minerals from the ground is called *mining*. Taking rocks from the ground is called *quarrying*.

Mining of minerals may take place on the surface of the ground or thousands of feet beneath it. In both cases, explosives are generally used to loosen the mineral deposits first. Deposits of coal and iron ore are sometimes mined on the surface. Large power shovels and other excavators dig out the loosened deposits. This is called *open-pit* or *open-cast* mining.

Another method of mining on the surface is *placer* mining. Gravel, in streams and in lakes, is dredged and sifted for heavy metal ores, such as gold, and precious stones, or gems. (See PLACERS.)

Gold and diamonds, for example, are mined deep underground. To reach them, deep shafts are drilled down into the ground,

This miner is pushing explosives into holes drilled in the rock. He will then detonate them, that is, set them off electrically, after he has moved to a safe place. The explosion will remove large sections of rock to reveal a coal seam, or mineral vein.

Mining bauxite, the ore of aluminium, in Australia. It is often found near the surface.

and tunnels are driven out from the shafts. The deepest mines are in South Africa.

Some minerals can be mined underground by different methods. Take sulphur, for example. Very hot, or *superheated* steam is used to melt the sulphur beneath the ground. Then high-pressure air forces the molten sulphur to the surface.

Quarrying of rocks is similar to surface mining in many ways, but explosives are used much more carefully. They must not, for example, break up valuable building stone into tiny pieces, otherwise it will be worthless. This method of blasting is needed for solid rock deposits, such as limestone and granite.

However, no explosives are needed for quarrying such deposits as sand, gravel, and shale. These deposits are naturally soft or loose. They can often be simply dug out by excavators. Sand and gravel pits soon fill with water, and dredgers must then be used to remove the deposits.

OBSIDIAN is a natural glass which forms when lava from a volcano cools rapidly. Most obsidian is jet-black. It is hard and breaks with sharp edges. For this reason, early man used obsidian to make tools and weapons. Obsidian is one of the igneous rocks. It is a solidified liquid, like glass. The same substances can be found as crystals in granite. (See GRANITE, IGNEOUS ROCK.)

Obsidian is sometimes called pitchstone because it looks rather like hard black tar, or pitch. It breaks in smooth sharp-edged curves, like flint, so it was used for prehistoric tools and weapons.

ORE Metals are extremely important to our present way of life. Only a few of them are found as metals in nature. They are the native metals gold, silver, copper and platinum. Most metals occur naturally in minerals in which they are combined with other chemical elements.

To be useful to man, the metals must be extracted from the minerals and purified. The minerals which can be treated to produce the pure metal are called *ores*.

The most common ores are *oxides*, compounds of the metals with oxygen; *carbonates*, compounds with carbon and oxygen; and *sulphides*, compounds with sulphur.

The ore minerals are not often used in their natural form, unlike the other minerals described in this book. They have to be processed before they become useful. For details about the main ores of the common metals, see BAUXITE (aluminium ore), CASSITERITE (tin ore), COPPER ORES, GALENA (lead ore), IRON ORES, and ZINC BLENDE.

PETRIFIED WOOD In northern Arizona, in the United States, you can see what appears to be a huge forest of felled trees; but if you touch the tree trunks, you will find that they are made of rock not wood. The wood has been *petrified*, or turned into stone. You can see similar petrified forests in other parts of the world, too.

The tree trunks turned into stone after they became buried under layers of mud and sand millions of years ago. Water containing stony minerals seeped into the trunks and gradually

Petrified wood. These ancient trees have been turned to stone. They have broken into sections on falling over, just like stone columns in a ruined building.

deposited the minerals in place of the rotting wood. In time, the whole structure of the wood was replaced and changed into stone.

PLACERS are deposits of heavy minerals which form in the beds of streams or on sea shores. Rocks crumble under the action of the weather, and the fragments are washed away by streams. The heavy minerals settle out before the lighter ones and gradually form into a deposit. Precious metals and gems are often found in these *stream* placers. *Beach* placers form when the sea washes away the light particles from the heavy minerals.

This model shows how valuable minerals are washed into stream placer deposits.

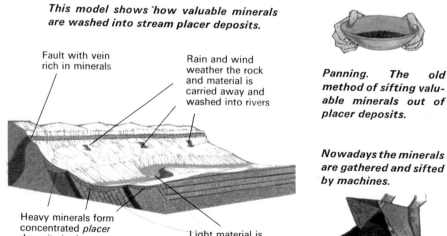

Fault with vein rich in minerals

Rain and wind weather the rock and material is carried away and washed into rivers

Heavy minerals form concentrated *placer* deposits in river gravels and sand

Light material is carried away by the river

Panning. The old method of sifting valuable minerals out of placer deposits.

Nowadays the minerals are gathered and sifted by machines.

PUMICE You probably have a piece of this kind of rock at home. You will know it better as the *pumice-stone* you use to remove hard pieces of skin or stains from your hands. Pumice is a kind of grey glass foam. It is so full of air bubbles that it floats on water.

Pumice is an igneous rock formed when molten lava from a volcano cools very quickly. Hot gases in the lava force their way through and puff up the cooling lava into a solid foam.

Pumice-stone is an igneous rock formed from lava which contained bubbles of gas.

PYRITES is one of the minerals which has often been mistaken for gold on account of its brassy yellow appearance. For this reason it is called 'fool's gold' It is actually a very common mineral containing iron and sulphur. It contains too much sulphur to be a useful iron ore, but it is a valuable source of sulphur. Also, many deposits of pyrites are rich in copper and gold.

Pyrites usually forms crystals of this shape.

The word *pyrites* means 'fire'. The mineral was given this name because sparks fly from it when you strike it with a hammer.

QUARTZ is one of the commonest of all minerals. It is one of the main minerals in the massive granite rocks which make up a great part of the Earth's surface. Sand and gravel are nearly all quartz.

Crystals of quartz are particularly beautiful. They are six-sided with pointed ends, just like a pencil stub sharpened at both ends. They appear in an astonishing variety of colours, and many of them are valued as semi-precious stones, or *gems*. (See GEMS.) They are valuable because they are hard as well as attractive.

The purest form of quartz is *rock crystal*, which is perfectly

47

Amethyst quartz, in crystal form and as the cut gem.

Two opaque forms of quartz which are used as ornamental stones.

clear. It has certain electrical properties which make it suitable for use in radio and telephone instruments. Quartz crystals become tinted in various attractive colours when they contain slight impurities.

One of the best quartz gems is *amethyst*, which is a beautiful violet; *citrin* is deep golden yellow; *rose quartz* is pale pink; *smoky quartz* (known as *cairngorm* in Scotland) is brownish-black.

The crystals in some quartz have not really developed properly, and the mineral becomes *opaque*, that is, it will not let light through. Attractive opaque forms of quartz include *agate* and *onyx*, which both have coloured bands in them. Agate has circular bands, and onyx has straight bands.

ROCKS We normally think of rocks as huge boulders or mountains made up of very hard material. In fact, rock is any kind of material which makes up the Earth's crust, or outer layer. It also includes soft materials like clay and sand. The study of rocks is called *petrology*.

Rock consists of substances which have a definite chemical make-up, or composition. These substances are called *minerals*. Some rocks, such as chalk, contain only one mineral. Other rocks, such as granite, contain two or more minerals.

In mountainous regions and at the seaside you often see slabs of bare rock rising above the ground. Elsewhere the solid rock lies beneath soft soil. You can often see this underlying rock when new roads are being cut through hillsides.

You may notice when looking at the exposed rock that it consists of a number of layers. This indicates that it is one of the main kinds of rock, *sedimentary* rock. This rock is formed from layer upon layer of material deposited years ago from rivers and seas. It is particularly interesting because it contains *fossils*, which are the remains of plants and animals. (See FOSSIL, SEDIMENTARY ROCK.)

48

The two other kinds of rock are *igneous* rock and *metamorphic* rock. They are often known as *massive* rocks because they are the same throughout. They do not have any noticeable layers like the sedimentary rocks. Igneous rocks are formed when molten material from inside the Earth cools at or near the surface. Metamorphic rocks are formed when igneous and sedimentary rocks are remelted due to heat and pressure and crystallize again. Most igneous and metamorphic rocks do not contain any fossils. (See IGNEOUS ROCK, METAMORPHIC ROCK.)

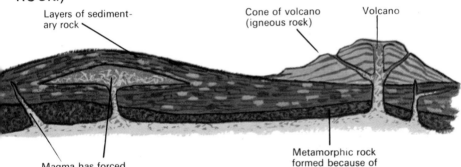

Layers of sediment-
ary rock

Cone of volcano
(igneous rock)

Volcano

Magma has forced
its way into cracks
and faults

Metamorphic rock
formed because of
pressure and heat
from the magma

ROCK SALT Most of our common table salt comes from massive deposits of *rock salt*. These deposits consist almost entirely of the mineral *halite*. They were formed millions of years ago when ancient seas dried up. Rock salt is really, then, a sedimentary rock.

We use salt for cooking and for preserving meats, for example. To remain healthy, we should eat more than ten pounds of salt a year. Farmers feed *salt-lick* to their cattle for the same reason. Most salt is used in industry to make a wide variety of chemicals, such as soda (for making glass) and chlorine (for purifying water).

Rock salt consists of a shiny solid mass, which may be white but is usually yellow, brown, or red. It looks quite different from the fine, pure white material we have on the dinner table.

Most rock salt is mined by pumping water through the deposits. The salt dissolves to form brine, which is pumped back to the surface. Some salt is, however, mined by men with machinery deep underground.

SAND is a common and very useful material. We use it, for example, to make glass and concrete. We find sand along most sea-shores. The constant pounding of the waves breaks up the rocks lining the shores. It grinds them into smaller and smaller pieces until they finally become grains of sand.

When the sand dries out, it can be easily blown about by the wind to form sand *dunes*. The dunes move across the land in slow waves. They can choke rivers and bury buildings. In the great sandy deserts of the world, the dunes are constantly in motion. Terrible blinding sandstorms can occur when the wind is strong.

Sand can contain a great many minerals, depending on the rock from which it was formed. The most common mineral in sand is *quartz*. (See QUARTZ.) Common sand is a yellowish-brown colour. The colour of sand may vary from pure white to jet black. The black sand is formed from volcanic rock.

Like clay, sand becomes cemented, or bound together, to form a hard, layered, or *sedimentary*, rock. This rock is called *sandstone*. It may vary in colour from white to yellow and red. The redness is caused by the presence of iron. Under great heat and pressure, sandstone will itself be changed into a rock called *quartzite*, which is one of the toughest of all rocks.

Sand grains
(magnified)

The waves are continually pounding at the cliffs and breaking off pieces of rock. These are ground together on the sea-bed until they are completely broken up and worn away to tiny fragments or sand. The sea carries the sand grains up onto the beach and gradually builds great dunes of sand.

SEDIMENTARY ROCK The gradual, but never-ending action of the weather breaks down even the hardest rocks into tiny particles. (See WEATHERING.) Streams carry the particles away and deposit them in another place. Over millions of years, layer upon layer builds up and gradually becomes cemented, or bound together, into a hard mass.

The kind of rock formed in this way is called *sedimentary* rock, because it is made up of layers of deposits, or *sediments.* It is also called *bedded* rock. The layers of rock are called *strata.* (See STRATA.)

Sedimentary rocks of this kind include sandstone made up of compressed sand, and shale made up of compressed clay. Rock formed when large pebbles and boulders are cemented together is called *conglomerate.*

Another kind of sedimentary rock is formed when minerals in the older rocks are gradually dissolved by water flowing over them. A stage is reached when the water can hold no more minerals, and the minerals begin to be deposited as crystals. They gradually form layers and eventually become rock-like. Rock salt and some limestones are sedimentary rocks of this kind. Some kinds of limestone consist mainly of the chalky remains of tiny sea creatures, such as coral.

Coal is a special kind of sedimentary rock. It was formed from plants which were buried in swamps and decayed. Pressure gradually changed the plant remains into the familiar hard black 'rock'.

Sedimentary rocks are very important because they contain a great many *fossils*, that is, plant and animal remains. Each layer in the rock formed at a different period in the Earth's history. By studying the fossils in the various layers, we can find out the order in which animals and plants appeared on Earth and how they developed. (See FOSSIL.)

The wind, the sea and the rivers all break off fragments of rock and carry them away. These fragments are cemented together when they are buried beneath land or water. The rock formed from them is called sedimentary rock.

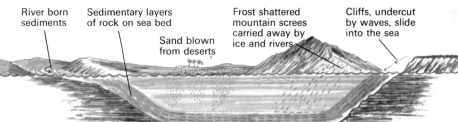

River born sediments

Sedimentary layers of rock on sea bed

Sand blown from deserts

Frost shattered mountain screes carried away by ice and rivers

Cliffs, undercut by waves, slide into the sea

SHALE Under certain conditions, layers of clay become pressed together to form a solid rock called *shale*. An important kind of shale is *oil-shale*. This is so called because it is soaked in oil. The oil can easily be obtained for fuel by heating the shale. Shale is a very common kind of sedimentary rock.

Shale is a sedimentary rock formed from layers of clay which have been pressed together. The coloured streaks show up the separate layers. The dark band may be soaked in oil.

SILICA AND SILICATES Silicon is one of the chemical elements, the 'building blocks' of nature. There is more silicon in the Earth's crust than any other element except oxygen. It is never found by itself, but is found combined with other elements, almost always with oxygen.

The simple combination of silicon with oxygen produces the common mineral *silica*. Sand, quartz crystals, and flint are all different forms of this mineral.

Even more common than silica are the complicated minerals called *silicates*. In these minerals, silicon is combined not only with oxygen, but also with one or more metallic elements. These elements include aluminium, iron, calcium, sodium and potassium. The commonest silicate mineral is feldspar, which is found in most of the original igneous rocks, such as granite. Other common silicates include clay and mica.

Crystals of tourmaline. It is a complicated silicate mineral containing aluminium and, sometimes, iron and magnesium.

Silica is used in the manufacture of glass. It is made by mixing pure sand, crushed quartz or broken flints with limestone and soda ash (obtained from salt) in a very hot furnace.

SLATE The roofs of some houses are covered with thin sheets of *slate*. A blackboard at school may also be made of slate. Slate is a metamorphic rock formed from shale which has been under great pressure. There are lines of weakness in the direction in which the pressure has acted, so it splits easily along these lines into thin, parallel sheets. The sheets of slate may have coloured streaks across them. These show how the shale was formed from successive layers of mud before it was compressed into slate. The mud itself may have come from different sources, as the water washed it away from older rocks. Different rocks produce mud in a variety of colours and so some slate may be red, green or purple although most of it is grey or black.

STALACTITES AND STALAGMITES Most limestone hills contain vast caverns hollowed out by underground rivers. The first thing you notice when you enter the caverns are the giant 'icicles' of stone hanging from the roof and stone columns rising from the floor.

Stalactites hang from the roofs of caves. They are made of calcite which is deposited as water drips from the roof. With each drop, the deposit grows a fraction larger. Stalagmites gradually grow up from the floor as a little more calcite is deposited there by each drip. The calcite comes from limestone which is dissolved as the water runs over the rock.

The 'icicles' are called *stalactites,* and the columns, *stalagmites*. They are formed by the constant dripping of water from the roof. The water dissolves quite a lot of limestone as it flows over the rocks. Every time it drips, a little of the limestone is deposited on the roof. A little more is deposited where it falls. Over many years the deposits grow into stalactites and stalagmites.

STRATA The most noticeable feature about sedimentary rocks is that they are made up of a number of layers, or *strata*.

These strata were more or less horizontal when they were first formed at the bottom of a river or sea. In some of the limestone cliffs you see today, the strata are still horizontal, but many of the sedimentary rocks have been pushed and twisted by movements of the Earth's crust. The strata show definite slopes, or *dips*. Some strata are even vertical. Many are bent into gentle curves, which are generally called *rock folds*.

Sometimes the strata did not bend but slipped vertically so that they are slightly out of step. This break in the strata is called a *fault*.

Line of *fault*

Strata which have been folded and faulted

Fresh sedimentary deposit

This was once a continuous horizontal layer

Sulphur occurs native and often grows into beautiful yellow crystals. This model shows their pyramid-like shape.

SULPHUR is a yellow mineral which is one of the chemical elements, the basic 'building blocks' of Nature. It is unusual because it melts at a temperature just above that of boiling water. Also, it burns and gives off choking 'sulphurous' fumes. These are the fumes you can smell when you go near a volcano. In fact, sulphur is deposited in and around the rocks near volcanoes, often in the form of beautiful crystals.

Sulphur is one of the most valuable

raw materials for the chemical industry. It is made first into sulphuric acid and then into many products, including large amounts of fertilizers. Sulphur itself is used for hardening, or *vulcanizing,* rubber for tyres. It is also used to make the gunpowder for fireworks.

Sulphur combines with metals to give compounds called *sulphides.* Pyrites is the commonest sulphide mineral. Many of the valuable ore minerals are sulphides. Galena (lead ore), zinc blende (zinc ore), chalcopyrite (copper ore), and cinnabar (mercury ore) are all sulphides.

TALC We come into contact with this mineral at a very early age, in the form of talcum powder. It is ideal for a baby's skin because it is one of the softest of all minerals. Baby powder accounts for only a small part of talc production. Very large amounts of talc are used in making pottery, paint, and paper.

Talc is sometimes called soapstone. It is very soft and feels greasy.

The great softness of talc makes it feel 'soapy'. For this reason the solid form of talc is often called *soapstone.* Tailors use small pieces of soapstone to mark cloth. They call it *French chalk.*

WEATHERING You can hardly imagine rocks wearing away by themselves. It is as much as you can do to break them with a hammer and chisel. But rocks do, in fact, wear away under the continual action of the weather. This process is called *weathering.*

Rain and sea water flowing over or pounding against rock gradually break it up and carry the particles away. Or they

The beautiful carving on a building may look like this when it is new, but after many years in the open air it is worn away. Chemicals in rain water attack the stone, grit in the wind grinds it away.

These strange sandstone pillars are an interesting feature of deserts. The strong winds blow sand against the remaining outcrops of rock and gradually wear them away, by 'sand blasting'. The uneven shapes are caused by the softer rock wearing away more quickly than the harder layers.

dissolve some of the minerals in the rock and cause it to crumble. Water seeps into cracks in the rock and expands when it freezes. This helps to force the rock apart. Hot sun during the day and frost at night eventually cause the rock to split.

These are all examples of the weathering that produces such fantastic shapes in nature. You cannot see much change in a single lifetime, but the effect is considerable over millions of years. Even the hardest granite rock will one day crumble away.

When the broken or dissolved rock is deposited, a new kind of rock begins to form. This is called a *sedimentary* rock. The process, of course, again takes millions of years.

Zinc blende, or sphalerite, is the chief source of zinc. It is a sulphide ore and is often found with galena.

ZINC BLENDE is the main ore of zinc. It is often called *sphalerite*. Both the words *blende* and *sphalerite* mean 'deceiving' or 'treacherous'. The mineral is called this because it is difficult to recognise and may resemble more valuable minerals, such as galena, a rich source of lead and silver. It may be almost white, golden, and even green, but it is usually brown or black. Like galena, zinc blende is a sulphide ore. (See ORE.)

Aids to Identifying Minerals

Hardness

One thing which helps us to identify a mineral is its hardness. The German mineralogist Friedrich Mohs suggested a scale in which well known minerals are placed in order of their hardness. He took talc – one of the softest minerals – as number 1 on his scale and diamond – the hardest mineral – as number 10. All the other minerals are classified in terms of this scale.

1. Talc	Crushed by finger nail
2. Gypsum	Scratched by finger nail
3. Calcite	Scratched by copper coin or iron nail
4. Fluorspar (Fluorite)	Scratched by glass
5. Apatite	Scratched by ordinary pen-knife blade
6. Feldspar	Scratched by quartz
7. Quartz	Scratched by hard steel file
8. Topaz	Scratched by corundum
9. Corundum (emerald, ruby, sapphire)	
10. Diamond	

Each mineral in the scale will scratch the one below it. For example, quartz (No. 7) will scratch feldspar (No. 6) and be scratched by topaz (No. 8). Minerals with the same hardness will scratch each other.

We find the position of a mineral in the scale by trying to scratch it with substances of known hardness. This is often known as the *scratch test*. When we go collecting minerals in the field, it would obviously be inconvenient (and expensive) to carry the ten minerals in the scale to scratch our specimens. We make do with a few simple objects of which we know the hardness:

Finger nail	$2\frac{1}{2}$	Penknife blade, glass	$5\frac{1}{2}$
Copper coin	3	Hard steel file	7

Arising from this, we can see that minerals with a hardness of less than $5\frac{1}{2}$ can be scratched by a knife, and that those with a hardness over $5\frac{1}{2}$ will scratch glass. Also it is worth remembering that minerals with a hardness less than $2\frac{1}{2}$ will mark paper.

The Mohs hardness of some common minerals are shown in the table on pages 58–59.

Lustre

The way in which a mineral reflects light is called its lustre. This is a property which is of great use in identifying minerals. We can divide them into two main groups — those with metallic and those with non-metallic lustres.

Minerals with a *metallic* lustre have the typical shine of a metal. Galena and pyrites are two of the many ore minerals which have metallic lustres.

There are several kinds of *non-metallic* lustres. The commonest is the *vitreous* (glass-like) lustre of quartz and many other minerals. Mica and other minerals that cleave (split) into thin, parallel layers have a *pearly* lustre. This is the typical rainbow-like appearance of a pearl, which is itself made up of thin layers.

Some minerals, such as asbestos and certain kinds of gypsum, are made up of tiny fibres. Their lustre is described as *silky*. Some lead minerals have the brilliant lustre of diamonds, called *adamantine*. Sulphur and zinc blende have *resinous* lustres — like the resin from pine trees.

Testing for Carbonates

Carbonates are among the commonest of the minerals. Chalk and limestone, for example, are made up mainly of calcite, which is calcium carbonate. Most carbonates are easy to recognize because they fizz, or give off bubbles of gas when acid is poured on them.

The acid geologists normally use is dilute hydrochloric acid. But you can often get similar results by using ordinary household vinegar, which is in fact a weak acid. The reaction will go more quickly if you test a little powder, scraped from your specimen with a knife blade.

Birthstones

Birthstones are gems which are related to the month of your birth. Wearing a birthstone is supposed to bring you luck. The birthstone of each month are shown below.

January	Garnet	July	Ruby
February	Amethyst	August	Peridot
March	Aquamarine	September	Sapphire
April	Diamond	October	Opal
May	Emerald	November	Topaz
June	Pearl or Moonstone	December	Turquoise or Zircon

MINERAL	COMPOSITION	COLOUR	HARDNESS
Azurite	Basic copper carbonate	Azure blue	$3\frac{1}{2}$–4
Barytes	Barium sulphate	White	3–$3\frac{1}{2}$
Beryl	Beryllium and aluminium silicates	Emerald, aquamarine	$7\frac{1}{2}$

MINERAL	COMPOSITION	COLOUR	HARDNESS
Calcite	Calcium carbonate	Colourless, various tints	3
Cassiterite	Tin oxide	Black	6–7
Chalcocite	Copper sulphide	Greyish-blue	$2\frac{1}{2}$–3
Chalcopyrites	Copper and iron sulphides	Brass yellow	$3\frac{1}{2}$–4
Cinnabar	Mercury sulphide	Vivid red	2–$2\frac{1}{2}$
Copper	Copper	Coppery red	$2\frac{1}{2}$–3
Corundum	Aluminium oxide	Sapphire blue, ruby red	9
Cryolite	Aluminium and sodium fluorides	Colourless, white	$2\frac{1}{2}$
Cuprite	Copper oxide	Reddish	$3\frac{1}{2}$–4
Diamond	Carbon	Colourless white	10
Dolomite	Calcium and magnesium carbonates	White, reddish brown	$3\frac{1}{2}$–4
Feldspar	Potassium, calcium, and sodium silicates	White, pink	6–$6\frac{1}{2}$
Fluorspar	Calcium fluoride	Blue, various	4
Galena	Lead sulphide	Lead-grey	$2\frac{1}{2}$
Garnet	Aluminium silicates	Red, purple	6–$7\frac{1}{2}$
Gold	Gold	Golden yellow	$2\frac{1}{2}$–3
Graphite	Carbon	Black	1–2
Gypsum	Calcium sulphate	White	2
Haematite	Iron oxide	Black, deep red	$5\frac{1}{2}$–$6\frac{1}{2}$
Halite	Sodium chloride	Colourless, white	$2\frac{1}{2}$
Limonite	Hydrated iron oxide	Brown	5–$5\frac{1}{2}$
Magnetite	Iron oxide	Greyish-black	6
Malachite	Basic copper carbonate	Bright green	$3\frac{1}{2}$–4
Mica (common)	Potassium and aluminium silicates	White	2–$2\frac{1}{2}$
Opal	Hydrated silica	Varied colours, rich 'play' of colours	$5\frac{1}{2}$
Pitchblende	Uranium dioxide	Black, greenish	$5\frac{1}{2}$
Pyrites	Iron sulphide	Brass yellow	6–$6\frac{1}{2}$
Pyrolusite	Manganese dioxide	Dark green	2
Quartz	Silicon dioxide	Colourless, various tints	7
Serpentine	Hydrated magnesium silicate	Usually mottled green	$2\frac{1}{2}$–4
Siderite	Iron carbonate	Brown	$3\frac{1}{2}$–4
Silver	Silver	Silver white	$2\frac{1}{2}$–3
Spinel	Magnesium and aluminium oxides	Red, blue, green	8
Sulphur	Sulphur	Yellow	$1\frac{1}{2}$–$2\frac{1}{2}$
Talc	Hydrated magnesium silicate	White, green	1
Topaz	Aluminium, fluorine silicate	Colourless, yellow, blue	8
Zinc blende	Zinc sulphide	Brown, black, red	4
Zircon	Zirconium silicate	Colourless, yellow, green	$7\frac{1}{2}$

● Index

Made and printed in Great Britain by Purnell & Sons Ltd.
Paulton (Somerset) and London

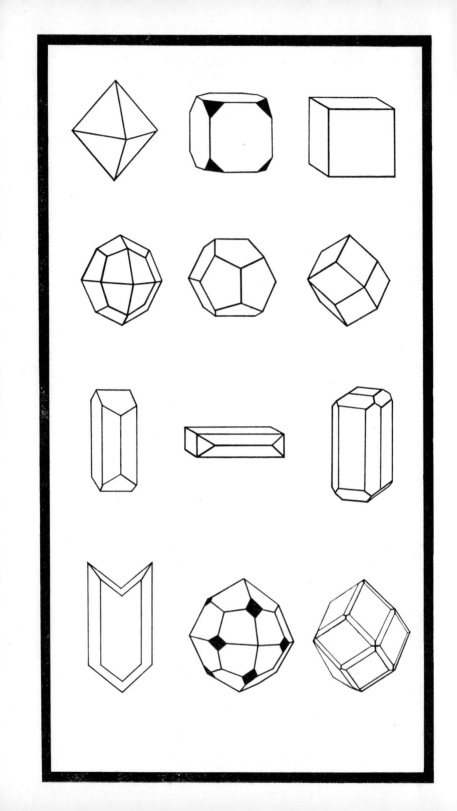